EMMANUEL JOSEPH

The Untethered Anchor, Balancing Stability and Adventure in a Changing World

Copyright © 2025 by Emmanuel Joseph

All rights reserved. No part of this publication may be reproduced, stored or transmitted in any form or by any means, electronic, mechanical, photocopying, recording, scanning, or otherwise without written permission from the publisher. It is illegal to copy this book, post it to a website, or distribute it by any other means without permission.

First edition

This book was professionally typeset on Reedsy.
Find out more at reedsy.com

Contents

1	Chapter 1: The Call to Adventure	1
2	Chapter 2: The Weight of Tradition	3
3	Chapter 3: Embracing Change	5
4	Chapter 4: The Role of Community	7
5	Chapter 5: The Anchor of Values	9
6	Chapter 6: The Quest for Knowledge	11
7	Chapter 7: Finding Balance in Relationships	13
8	Chapter 8: The Art of Mindfulness	15
9	Chapter 9: The Power of Resilience	17
10	Chapter 10: Navigating Uncertainty	19
11	Chapter 11: The Pursuit of Passion	21
12	Chapter 12: Embracing Diversity	23
13	Chapter 13: Cultivating Creativity	25
14	Chapter 14: The Journey of Self-Discovery	27
15	Chapter 15: The Importance of Rest and Renewal	29
16	Chapter 16: The Dance of Change	31
17	Chapter 17: The Legacy of the Untethered Anchor	33

1

Chapter 1: The Call to Adventure

In every person's life, there comes a moment when the familiar begins to feel constricting and the unknown beckons like a siren's call. The initial tug of wanderlust can be exhilarating and terrifying in equal measure, as it whispers promises of new experiences and untapped potential. For many, this is the beginning of a journey that will redefine their very existence. It starts with the realization that while stability brings comfort, it can also breed stagnation. To truly grow, one must occasionally break free from the anchor of routine and embrace the uncharted waters of adventure.

The desire for adventure is often born out of a deep-seated need for change. This need can manifest in various ways: a longing for new environments, the pursuit of knowledge, or the quest for personal development. It is this intrinsic motivation that propels individuals to step beyond their comfort zones and explore the world beyond. The journey may be daunting, but the rewards are immeasurable. With each new experience, one gains a deeper understanding of oneself and the world, forging a path toward self-discovery and fulfillment.

Yet, the allure of adventure must be balanced with the necessity of stability. While the thrill of the unknown can be intoxicating, it is the anchor of routine that provides the foundation upon which one can build. Stability offers a sense of security, a place to return to when the tides of change become overwhelming. It is this delicate balance between the two that allows one to navigate the ever-changing currents of life with grace and resilience. The key lies in finding harmony between the call to adventure and the anchor of stability.

Ultimately, the journey toward balancing stability and adventure is a deeply personal one. Each individual must chart their course, guided by their unique desires and aspirations. It is a journey that requires courage, introspection, and a willingness to embrace uncertainty. But for those who dare to embark on this path, the rewards are boundless. The untethered anchor becomes a symbol of freedom, a testament to the power of embracing both stability and adventure in a changing world.

2

Chapter 2: The Weight of Tradition

Tradition serves as an anchor, grounding us in cultural heritage and communal values. It provides a sense of belonging and identity, fostering connections to our ancestors and the wisdom of the past. However, the weight of tradition can also be restrictive, stifling individuality and discouraging innovation. Balancing the preservation of tradition with the pursuit of personal and societal progress is a delicate act that requires introspection and courage.

As we navigate the changing currents of the modern world, it becomes essential to critically examine the traditions we uphold. Are they serving our growth and well-being, or are they merely relics of a bygone era? The challenge lies in discerning which aspects of tradition enhance our lives and which ones hinder our potential. By embracing the valuable lessons of the past while remaining open to new possibilities, we can forge a path that honors our heritage while fostering personal and collective evolution.

One way to balance tradition with progress is through adaptive innovation. This involves reinterpreting traditional practices in ways that are relevant to contemporary contexts. By doing so, we can preserve the core values and wisdom embedded in these practices while making them more accessible and meaningful to future generations. Adaptive innovation allows us to maintain a connection to our roots while embracing the dynamic nature of the world around us.

Ultimately, the weight of tradition should not be a burden but a source of strength. By thoughtfully integrating tradition into our lives, we can create a sense of continuity and stability that anchors us as we explore new horizons. The untethered anchor becomes a symbol of our ability to honor the past while boldly stepping into the future, balancing the wisdom of tradition with the spirit of adventure.

3

Chapter 3: Embracing Change

Change is an inevitable part of life, and our ability to adapt to it often determines our success and fulfillment. While stability offers a sense of security, it is through embracing change that we experience growth and transformation. The journey of balancing stability and adventure requires a mindset that is open to the unknown and willing to take risks. It is in the face of change that we discover our true potential and resilience.

Embracing change involves letting go of the familiar and stepping into the uncertain. This can be challenging, as it requires us to confront our fears and vulnerabilities. However, it is through this process that we develop a deeper understanding of ourselves and our capabilities. Change presents opportunities for learning, growth, and reinvention, allowing us to continually evolve and adapt to new circumstances.

One of the keys to embracing change is cultivating a flexible mindset. This involves being open to new ideas, perspectives, and experiences, and being willing to adjust our plans and goals as needed. Flexibility allows us to navigate the unpredictable nature of life with grace and resilience, transforming challenges into opportunities for growth. By remaining adaptable, we can harness the power of change to propel us forward on our journey.

At the core of embracing change is the recognition that life is a dynamic and ever-evolving journey. By letting go of the need for control and certainty, we can fully embrace the adventure of living. The untethered anchor symbolizes our ability to navigate the changing currents of life with a sense of curiosity and wonder, balancing the stability of the known with the excitement of the unknown.

4

Chapter 4: The Role of Community

Community plays a vital role in our journey of balancing stability and adventure. It provides a support system that anchors us during times of uncertainty and change. Within a community, we find connection, belonging, and a shared sense of purpose. These relationships offer stability and security, creating a foundation upon which we can embark on our individual adventures.

The strength of a community lies in its diversity and collective wisdom. By fostering inclusive and supportive environments, communities can nurture personal growth and innovation. They provide a safe space for individuals to explore their passions, take risks, and pursue their dreams. In turn, individuals contribute their unique talents and perspectives, enriching the community as a whole.

However, the role of community extends beyond support and stability. It also serves as a catalyst for adventure and exploration. Within a community, we find inspiration and encouragement to step outside our comfort zones and embrace new experiences. The collective energy and enthusiasm of a community can ignite our sense of curiosity and drive, propelling us toward new horizons.

Balancing stability and adventure within a community involves fostering a culture of trust and collaboration. This requires open communication, empathy, and a willingness to embrace change together. By working collectively to navigate the challenges and opportunities of life, communities can create an environment that supports both individual and collective growth. The untethered anchor becomes a symbol of the strength and resilience found in unity, as we journey together toward a future filled with possibility and adventure.

5

Chapter 5: The Anchor of Values

Our values serve as the guiding principles that anchor us in the face of life's uncertainties. They shape our decisions, influence our actions, and define our character. In a rapidly changing world, holding onto our core values provides a sense of stability and purpose. However, it is equally important to remain open to reevaluating and evolving our values as we grow and learn.

The process of defining and refining our values involves deep introspection and self-awareness. By examining what truly matters to us, we can identify the principles that resonate with our authentic selves. These values become the compass that guides us through the challenges and opportunities of life, helping us stay true to our path even when external circumstances shift.

Balancing stability and adventure requires a commitment to living in alignment with our values while remaining adaptable to change. This means being willing to question and challenge our beliefs, and making adjustments when necessary. By doing so, we can ensure that our values remain relevant and meaningful, allowing us to navigate the complexities of life with integrity and grace.

Ultimately, our values are the foundation upon which we build our lives. They provide a sense of continuity and stability that anchors us as we explore new horizons. The untethered anchor symbolizes our ability to stay grounded in our values while embracing the dynamic nature of the world, balancing the steadfastness of our principles with the openness to growth and transformation.

6

Chapter 6: The Quest for Knowledge

Knowledge is a powerful tool that empowers us to navigate the world with confidence and curiosity. The pursuit of knowledge fuels our sense of adventure, driving us to explore new ideas, cultures, and experiences. At the same time, a solid foundation of knowledge provides the stability needed to make informed decisions and approach challenges with wisdom.

The quest for knowledge is an ongoing journey that requires an open and inquisitive mind. It involves seeking out new information, questioning assumptions, and being willing to learn from a variety of sources. By embracing a mindset of lifelong learning, we can continuously expand our understanding of the world and ourselves, enriching our lives with new perspectives and insights.

Balancing stability and adventure in the pursuit of knowledge involves integrating formal education with experiential learning. While academic institutions provide a structured environment for acquiring knowledge, real-world experiences offer valuable opportunities for hands-on exploration and discovery. By combining these approaches, we can cultivate a well-rounded and dynamic understanding of the world.

Ultimately, the quest for knowledge is a journey of both personal and collective growth. It allows us to develop the skills and insights needed to navigate the complexities of life, while also contributing to the advancement of society. The untethered anchor symbolizes our ability to remain rooted in a strong foundation of knowledge while embracing the endless possibilities of discovery and exploration.

7

Chapter 7: Finding Balance in Relationships

Relationships are a fundamental aspect of the human experience, providing connection, support, and companionship. They anchor us in times of need and enhance our sense of belonging. However, relationships can also be a source of conflict and stress, requiring careful navigation to maintain harmony and balance.

Finding balance in relationships involves understanding and respecting the needs and boundaries of both ourselves and others. It requires open communication, empathy, and a willingness to compromise. By fostering healthy and supportive relationships, we can create a stable foundation that allows us to explore new experiences and pursue our individual goals.

At the same time, relationships should not be a source of limitation or restriction. It is important to cultivate connections that encourage growth, independence, and adventure. By surrounding ourselves with individuals who support and inspire us, we can embark on our journeys with confidence and enthusiasm, knowing that we have a strong network to return to.

Ultimately, balancing stability and adventure in relationships involves nurturing connections that provide both security and freedom. The untethered anchor symbolizes our ability to maintain healthy and fulfilling relationships while embracing the excitement of new experiences. By cultivating a balance between connection and independence, we can navigate the ever-changing landscape of life with grace and resilience.

8

Chapter 8: The Art of Mindfulness

Mindfulness is the practice of being present in the moment, fully engaged with our thoughts, feelings, and surroundings. It is a powerful tool for balancing stability and adventure, as it allows us to cultivate a sense of inner peace and awareness. By embracing mindfulness, we can navigate the complexities of life with greater clarity and intention.

The art of mindfulness involves developing a heightened sense of awareness and acceptance of the present moment. This practice can be cultivated through various techniques, such as meditation, deep breathing, and mindful observation. By incorporating mindfulness into our daily lives, we can create a sense of stability and calm amidst the chaos of the external world.

At the same time, mindfulness can enhance our sense of adventure by helping us fully appreciate and engage with new experiences. By being present and attentive, we can savor the richness of each moment, deepening our connection to the world and ourselves. Mindfulness encourages us to approach life with curiosity and openness, transforming ordinary experiences into extraordinary ones.

Ultimately, the art of mindfulness is a journey of self-discovery and growth. It allows us to find balance between stability and adventure, cultivating a sense of inner calm while embracing the excitement of new possibilities. The untethered anchor symbolizes our ability to stay grounded in the present moment while navigating the ever-changing currents of life with mindfulness and grace.

9

Chapter 9: The Power of Resilience

Resilience is the ability to bounce back from adversity and adapt to life's challenges. It is a crucial quality for balancing stability and adventure, as it allows us to navigate the ups and downs of our journey with grace and strength. By cultivating resilience, we can face the uncertainties of life with confidence, knowing that we have the inner resources to overcome obstacles and thrive.

Building resilience involves developing a positive mindset and a sense of self-efficacy. This means recognizing our strengths and capabilities, and believing in our ability to handle difficult situations. It also involves learning from setbacks and failures, viewing them as opportunities for growth and improvement. By embracing a resilient mindset, we can approach life's challenges with optimism and determination.

Another key aspect of resilience is building a strong support network. Surrounding ourselves with supportive and encouraging individuals can provide the emotional and practical assistance needed to navigate tough times. By fostering positive relationships and seeking out sources of support, we can enhance our resilience and create a stable foundation from which to explore new adventures.

Ultimately, the power of resilience lies in our ability to adapt and grow in the face of adversity. By cultivating resilience, we can find balance between stability and adventure, navigating the changing currents of life with strength and confidence. The untethered anchor symbolizes our ability to remain steadfast and resilient, even as we embrace the excitement and uncertainty of new experiences.

10

Chapter 10: Navigating Uncertainty

Uncertainty is an inherent part of the human experience, and our ability to navigate it plays a significant role in our overall well-being. While stability offers a sense of predictability and control, it is through embracing uncertainty that we can discover new opportunities and possibilities. The journey of balancing stability and adventure requires a mindset that is comfortable with ambiguity and open to the unknown.

Navigating uncertainty involves developing a sense of inner security and trust in ourselves. This means having confidence in our ability to handle whatever comes our way and believing in our capacity to adapt and thrive. By cultivating a strong sense of self, we can approach uncertain situations with a sense of calm and assurance, knowing that we have the inner resources to navigate the unknown.

Another important aspect of navigating uncertainty is embracing a sense of curiosity and openness. Rather than fearing the unknown, we can approach it with a sense of wonder and excitement, viewing it as an opportunity for growth and discovery. By adopting a curious mindset, we can transform uncertainty into a source of inspiration and creativity, allowing us to explore new horizons with enthusiasm.

Ultimately, navigating uncertainty is about finding balance between control and surrender. While it is important to have a sense of direction and purpose, it is equally important to remain open to the unexpected twists and turns of life. The untethered anchor symbolizes our ability to navigate uncertainty with grace and resilience, balancing the stability of our inner security with the adventure of the unknown.

11

Chapter 11: The Pursuit of Passion

Passion is the driving force that fuels our sense of adventure and purpose. It is the fire that ignites our creativity, motivation, and enthusiasm, propelling us toward our dreams and goals. At the same time, a strong sense of passion provides a sense of stability and fulfillment, anchoring us in the pursuit of our aspirations.

The pursuit of passion involves identifying what truly excites and inspires us. This requires deep introspection and self-awareness, as well as a willingness to explore new interests and experiences. By discovering our passions, we can create a sense of purpose and direction that guides us on our journey, providing the motivation and energy needed to overcome challenges and pursue our dreams.

Balancing stability and adventure in the pursuit of passion involves integrating our passions into our daily lives. This means finding ways to pursue our interests and goals while maintaining a sense of balance and well-being. By creating a harmonious blend of work, play, and rest, we can cultivate a fulfilling and dynamic life that honors both our passions and our need for stability.

Ultimately, the pursuit of passion is a journey of self-discovery and growth. It allows us to tap into our inner fire and unleash our full potential, creating a life that is rich with meaning and adventure. The untethered anchor symbolizes our ability to remain grounded in our passions while embracing the excitement and possibilities of the world, balancing the stability of our purpose with the adventure of our dreams.

12

Chapter 12: Embracing Diversity

Diversity is a fundamental aspect of the human experience, enriching our lives with a multitude of perspectives, cultures, and ideas. Embracing diversity allows us to broaden our horizons and deepen our understanding of the world, fostering a sense of curiosity and empathy. At the same time, a diverse and inclusive environment provides a stable foundation for personal and collective growth.

Embracing diversity involves recognizing and valuing the unique contributions of individuals from different backgrounds and experiences. This requires an open and inclusive mindset, as well as a commitment to creating equitable and supportive environments. By celebrating diversity, we can create a sense of belonging and connection that enhances our sense of stability and community.

At the same time, diversity fosters a spirit of adventure and exploration. By engaging with different cultures, ideas, and perspectives, we can expand our understanding of the world and challenge our assumptions. This process of discovery and learning allows us to grow and evolve, transforming our lives with new insights and experiences.

Ultimately, embracing diversity is about finding balance between unity and individuality. It involves creating a sense of community and connection while honoring the unique contributions of each individual. The untethered anchor symbolizes our ability to navigate the rich tapestry of human diversity with openness and curiosity, balancing the stability of our shared humanity with the adventure of discovering new perspectives.

13

Chapter 13: Cultivating Creativity

Creativity is the lifeblood of innovation and exploration. It fuels our sense of adventure, enabling us to think beyond the boundaries of convention and imagine new possibilities. At the same time, a strong foundation of creative expression provides a sense of stability and fulfillment, enriching our lives with meaning and joy.

Cultivating creativity involves embracing a mindset of curiosity and openness. This means being willing to experiment, take risks, and explore new ideas without fear of failure. By fostering a sense of playfulness and wonder, we can tap into our innate creative potential and unlock new avenues for growth and discovery.

Balancing stability and adventure in the cultivation of creativity involves creating an environment that nurtures and supports creative expression. This can include setting aside dedicated time for creative pursuits, seeking out inspiration from diverse sources, and surrounding ourselves with individuals who encourage and inspire us. By integrating creativity into our daily lives, we can create a sense of harmony and balance that enhances our overall well-being.

Ultimately, the cultivation of creativity is a journey of self-expression and growth. It allows us to explore new horizons, challenge our assumptions, and transform our lives with the power of imagination. The untethered anchor symbolizes our ability to remain grounded in our creative essence while embracing the excitement and possibilities of the world, balancing the stability of our inner creativity with the adventure of new ideas.

14

Chapter 14: The Journey of Self-Discovery

Self-discovery is a lifelong journey that involves exploring the depths of our inner world and uncovering the essence of who we are. It is a process of introspection, reflection, and growth, allowing us to develop a deeper understanding of ourselves and our place in the world. By embarking on the journey of self-discovery, we can find balance between stability and adventure, creating a life that is rich with meaning and purpose.

The journey of self-discovery involves embracing a mindset of curiosity and openness. This means being willing to explore our thoughts, feelings, and experiences, and being open to learning and growth. By cultivating self-awareness, we can gain insight into our strengths, weaknesses, values, and aspirations, allowing us to make more informed and authentic choices.

Balancing stability and adventure in the journey of self-discovery involves creating a sense of inner stability while remaining open to new experiences and possibilities. This can include practices such as journaling, meditation, and self-reflection, which provide a stable foundation for exploring our inner world. At the same time, it is important to seek out new experiences and challenges that push us beyond our comfort zones and encourage growth.

Ultimately, the journey of self-discovery is a path of continuous growth and evolution. It allows us to uncover our true potential, embrace our authentic selves, and create a life that is aligned with our deepest desires and values. The untethered anchor symbolizes our ability to remain grounded in our inner truth while embracing the adventure of self-discovery, balancing the stability of our core essence with the excitement of new possibilities.

15

Chapter 15: The Importance of Rest and Renewal

Rest and renewal are essential aspects of maintaining balance in our lives. They provide the stability and rejuvenation needed to sustain our sense of adventure and creativity. By prioritizing rest and self-care, we can create a strong foundation of well-being that supports our overall growth and fulfillment.

The importance of rest and renewal lies in their ability to restore our physical, mental, and emotional energy. This can include practices such as sleep, relaxation, and mindfulness, which allow us to recharge and reset. By taking the time to rest and renew, we can prevent burnout and maintain a sense of balance and vitality in our lives.

Balancing stability and adventure in the context of rest and renewal involves integrating self-care practices into our daily routines. This means creating a healthy balance between work, play, and rest, and being mindful of our needs and boundaries. By prioritizing self-care, we can create a stable foundation that supports our sense of adventure and exploration.

Ultimately, the importance of rest and renewal lies in their ability to enhance our overall well-being and resilience. They allow us to navigate the challenges and opportunities of life with greater clarity, energy, and enthusiasm. The untethered anchor symbolizes our ability to remain grounded in our well-being while embracing the excitement and possibilities of the world, balancing the stability of rest and renewal with the adventure of new experiences.

16

Chapter 16: The Dance of Change

Change is a constant and dynamic force that shapes our lives in profound ways. The dance of change involves finding harmony between stability and adventure, allowing us to navigate the ever-changing currents of life with grace and resilience. By embracing the dance of change, we can create a life that is rich with growth, discovery, and fulfillment.

The dance of change requires a mindset of adaptability and flexibility. This means being open to new experiences, perspectives, and opportunities, and being willing to adjust our plans and goals as needed. By cultivating a sense of fluidity and openness, we can navigate the complexities of life with ease and grace, transforming challenges into opportunities for growth.

Balancing stability and adventure in the dance of change involves creating a sense of inner stability that anchors us amidst the shifting tides of life. This can include practices such as mindfulness, self-reflection, and goal-setting, which provide a stable foundation for navigating change. At the same time, it is important to embrace the excitement and possibilities of the unknown, allowing us to explore new horizons and discover our true potential.

Ultimately, the dance of change is a journey of continuous growth and evolution. It allows us to adapt and thrive in the face of life's uncertainties, creating a life that is dynamic, resilient, and fulfilling. The untethered anchor symbolizes our ability to navigate the dance of change with grace and resilience, balancing the stability of our inner foundation with the adventure of the unknown.

17

Chapter 17: The Legacy of the Untethered Anchor

The legacy of the untethered anchor is one of balance, resilience, and adventure. It represents our ability to navigate the complexities of life with grace and confidence, finding harmony between stability and exploration. By embracing the principles of the untethered anchor, we can create a life that is rich with meaning, purpose, and fulfillment.

The legacy of the untethered anchor involves cultivating a sense of inner stability and strength. This means developing a strong foundation of values, self-awareness, and resilience that anchors us amidst the changing currents of life. By nurturing our inner stability, we can navigate the challenges and opportunities of life with greater ease and confidence.

At the same time, the legacy of the untethered anchor involves embracing a spirit of adventure and exploration. This means being open to new experiences, perspectives, and possibilities, and being willing to step beyond our comfort zones. By fostering a sense of curiosity and wonder, we can create a life that is dynamic, vibrant, and fulfilling.

Ultimately, the legacy of the untethered anchor is a journey of continuous growth and evolution. It allows us to find balance between stability and adventure, creating a life that is rich with meaning, purpose, and fulfillment. The untethered anchor symbolizes our ability to navigate the complexities of life with grace and resilience, balancing the stability of our inner foundation with the adventure of new horizons.

Book Description: The Untethered Anchor: Balancing Stability and Adventure in a Changing World

In a world constantly evolving, the desire to break free from the chains of routine and explore the unknown is an intrinsic part of the human experience. *The Untethered Anchor: Balancing Stability and Adventure in a Changing World* delves into the delicate equilibrium between the need for stability and the yearning for adventure. This captivating book explores the journey of embracing change, cultivating resilience, and finding harmony in the dance of life.

Through seventeen thought-provoking chapters, readers are invited to explore themes such as the weight of tradition, the power of community, the pursuit of passion, and the art of mindfulness. Each chapter offers a blend of introspective insights and practical guidance, encouraging readers to navigate the complexities of life with grace and confidence.

The book emphasizes the importance of grounding oneself in core values while remaining open to new experiences and possibilities. It provides a roadmap for personal growth, self-discovery, and the cultivation of creativity, all while fostering a sense of inner peace and stability. Readers will learn to embrace diversity, nurture healthy relationships, and harness the power of rest and renewal as they embark on their unique journeys.

The Untethered Anchor is a compelling guide for anyone seeking to balance the steadfastness of stability with the excitement of adventure. It is a testament to the power of resilience, adaptability, and the courage to explore new horizons. Whether you are at the beginning of your journey or well along the path, this book offers invaluable wisdom and inspiration for navigating the ever-changing world with a sense of purpose and fulfillment.

www.ingramcontent.com/pod-product-compliance
Lightning Source LLC
LaVergne TN
LVHW020500080526
838202LV00057B/6059